The Post-Pandemic Planet

Harish Kumar

Published by Harish Kumar, 2020.

THE POST-PANDEMIC PLANET

First edition. June 8, 2020.

Copyright © 2020 Harish Kumar.

ISBN: 978-1393246848

Written by Harish Kumar.

Table of Contents

Preface

The Covid-19 pandemic is wreaking widespread disruption, social and economic. Much more than what the Great Depression and the Second World War together did. Unfolding as humankind's greatest challenge to date, the pandemic is rapidly altering the world, its politics and economics. In the process, turning upside down established relationships, accepted rules and prevalent norms.

Though we cannot foretell with certainty what is in store, we can at least try to decode the telltale signs that are popping up all around us. *The Post-Pandemic Planet* does precisely that.

This futuristic study examines the socio-cultural changes that are in the offing. It peeps through the prism of unfolding events to understand the possibilities that lie ahead.

Among others, *The Post-Pandemic Planet* looks at how coercion-employing territorial states are changing and how the politico-cultural nation states are morphing. It tries to go into the reasons why our social lives are gradually getting colonised and why mysophobia will increasingly dictate the complexion of travel tomorrow.

Is Covidisation of a new European Union a possibility? What happens to the concept of common markets now? Will the Marshalls and the Molotovs give way to the Merkels of the world? Will food nationalism degenerate into gastroracism?

What colour the world health order is likely to take? How will the dissent-intolerant governments manipulate the privacy laws tomorrow? Why is the World Wide Web in the danger of turning into a World Narrow Web? Will jingoistic data localisation lead to digital dictatorships?

These are among a score of questions you will find answered in *The Post-Pandemic Planet*. As a pandemic-threatened planetarian, you are sure to find them absorbing.

1 The Data Deluge

The rising wave is set to turn into a deluge. Even after the locked-down denizens of this world emerge out of their cramped cocoons of compulsive quarantine, the Internet data wave would only go on to rise. Rise higher than ever before, only to become a deluge.

Today, the people of this planet may sulkingly remain hunkered down, out of force. Tomorrow too, they would, wherever and whenever possible, choose to remain so. Out of will this time. As this trend of self-quarantining expected to gather steam, you should see the Internet data stream hitting volumes.

Consider these pieces of data to prove that point. Verizon, the largest fibre provider in United States increased recently its 2020 capital expenditure guidance by 500 million US Dollars to 18.5 billion US Dollars to hasten its 5G avatar.

According to another piece of data, released by the web services company Cloudfare, Internet data traffic moved up by 18 per cent during the three months running up to March 2020 in United States. Luckily, the Internet architecture is designed to withstand sudden spikes in data traffic. So, now sweat, post-Corona.

As the usage frequency of social media set to rise further, as all things educational poised to move rapidly online post-Corona, as entertainment could come to depend largely on content providers like Netflix, as Internet banking is certain to be seen as the new normal and as online shopping should rise further, do not expect Internet data traffic to move Southward. Post-Corona, Internet data flow could only get thicker and faster.

With a global computer network like the Internet right on your palms or on the table facing you, the temptation to taste the assorted offerings of information through interconnected networks will certainly grow higher. Strange are the ways of habits and temptations.

So, what kind of projections you can see for the continued rise in Internet data usage post-Corona?

The Cisco Annual Internet Report 2018-2023 White Paper updated on 9 March 2020 has the answer: nearly two-thirds of the global population will have Internet access by 2023. By then, there will be 5.3 billion total Internet users, working out to 66 percent of global population, up from 3.9 billion in 2018. Even in the darkest region Africa-Middle East, there will be 611 million Internet users by 2023, up from 381 million in 2018.

Well, post-Corona, a larger number of young learners will learn more through enterprise communication channels like Google Hangouts. A bevy of housewives will fall in fiery love with online cooking recipes. More and more writers will rejoice in increasing their e-publishing frequency.

As larger packs of consumers discover the heightened pleasures of online shopping, a slew of banking customers will find it hard to forego the joys of e-banking discovered during the difficult Covid phase. And of course we have the ever-addictive social media, which will see greater usage and spike in the number of Internet users. Sure, addiction will prove to be more addictive.

That is why Cisco's projection for 2023 that spells out the total number of global Internet users rising at a compounded annual growth rate of 6 percent should come true, faster post-Corona. In people-percentage terms, the number that works out to 51 per cent of the global population in 2018 could turn larger tomorrow. There is every possibility of this coming data deluge may result in what could be termed as Data Digestive Disorder.

With more countries expected to hasten their hop on to the much-needed 5G bandwagon post-Corona, Cisco may not be off the mark.

2 Omnipresent Online Economy

Offline to online. Expect that slow transition to become faster now post-Corona. The smartphones we hold in our hands as a constant ally will surely double up as Super Duper Computers, aiding that transition to go forward at full throttle.

As and when the deadly Corona disappears from the scene, the digital economy, the online economy as business economists term it, will be before us in a larger-than-life avatar. Evidences of that are visible in the giddy valuation of the videoconferencing entity Zoom and in the mushrooming of online courses offered by almost every American university.

Already online Goliaths like Amazon, Google, Facebook and Alibaba are household names and more of their ilk will become mega digital companies, thus lengthening today's list of 67 largest Internet companies. These companies straddle a host of sectors from entertainment to ePublishing, transport to technology, retailing to ride-hailing, and entertainment to ePayment, among others.

Well, you might argue digital economy is already there as evidenced by these 67 mega Internet companies. Well, the Internet Goliaths will get much bigger, raising concerns among monopoly-bashers and oligopoly-haters. Bad luck for them, many more medium to large Internet companies with market dominance will appear on the online scene.

This digital economy, however, will transform into a larger economic identity, to include the entire online ecosystem and the whole community of interacting organisms along with their environment. That means a sudden spatial implosion, followed by an exponential growth and explosion in the digital space.

According to one estimate half the world's population today is online, a third are on a social network and again a half on mobile. These online-led weaning creatures will be seen more scattered across this planet.

Do not expect these online-addicted animals to be confined to certain age groups, select clusters of communities, definite comity of nations and cultures. They will be seen sprayed everywhere.

Such a climactic explosion in people connectivity and Online Omnipresence will lead to an exponential expansion of the digital economy.

You will see such a digital economy maturing into a three-trillion-dollar-plus ecosystem driven by innovations in digital technology, more robust digital infrastructure, more intuitive digital devices, hyperactive online user networks, mammoth animals of digital advertising and mega sources of digital content supply.

Outrageous social media channels, pervasive mobile Internet and intrusive digital advertising will complement them.

With the work-safely-at-home culture set to get accepted wider, the dictum of the post-pandemic environment will be simply this: Be online or be off course.

3 On-Demand App Autocracy

Chaos first, the rebirth later. That will be the brief story of the music and the entertainment industries, Corona to post-Corona. The chaos is primarily due to the infection-curbing moves by governments to control crowds and mass gatherings during the outbreak phase.

That means bidding adieu to cheering crowds and swelling stadia. With concert tours out of question, the music industry is going almost bust. The rise of digital piracy is just tailor-made to deliver a double whammy.

All that could change post-Corona. Hastened by the birth of digital streaming platforms at temptingly low subscription rates round the year, you may see the music industry experiencing a resurgence post-Corona. By keeping music streams running, the social media exposure of music artistes might be widened. That should help artistes earn better and digital music turn more popular.

Post-Corona, you may also witness a scenario wherein fan-funded music projects take off in a big way. These crowdfunded projects are likely to be aided in large measure by music-dedicated platforms like ArtistShare.com, Patreon.com and PledgeMusic.com. You may even see a spike in the number of such platforms catalysing the resurgence in the music industry.

Such will be the vigour of resurgence in music, vintage and modern, vinyl records might swing back to charm music-lovers, evoking nostalgia and memories in the run up. Why, photoshopped music melas might even enthral music maniacs.

This online music industry rejuvenation could turn out to be a remodelling moment for offline music, whenever and in whatever scale that happens. For instance, Stockholm-based global music streaming platform Spotify plans to face the post-pandemic world with emphasis, greater on on-demand listening and lower on linear programming.

All through this, the signs of resurgence in the music industry are already evident. Spotify, for instance, has been experiencing, of late, a rebound in its listening metrics. In red-hot Corona-hit regions like Italy and Spain, Spotify might be witnessing a decline in the number of daily active users. But, Spotify listening has been on the rebound elsewhere.

The message from Spotify founder and CEO Daniel Ek sums it all up. He is saying the everything-linear trend will die a slow death and everything-on-demand will win hands down. This is a trend that might get the push post-pandemic. When that trend ushers in App Autocracy, audience would turn apostles of content consumption.

In the entertainment industry too, you are sure to see lasting changes in how you watch and pay for content. These changes will be hastened by the emergence of Netflix copycats. The focus will largely be on online streaming. And business models will be built around such models. Why not, if Netflix are earnings are more than annual box office collections?

Post-Corona, movie theatre chains may phase themselves out, the weaker ones particularly. These minnows may get swallowed by the exhibition sharks. Or, just disappear. Even when surviving theatres reopen for business, the affinity to online streaming and viewing will continue. That is how habits develop.

Such addictive streaming may lead to lull in movie production, creating scarcity of new content for streaming. Plus, easy access to free user-generated content on social media apps could force even streaming services into a fix.

That apart, cable TV packages will die a slow death thanks to cheaper streaming alternatives. The warning signals are already blinking. Some production houses in America and elsewhere have put a few upcoming film releases on hold, and why, many are converting themselves to on-demand rental services. That means apps with their own paywalls will be the new normal in the entertainment sector post-Corona.

The moot question that will always remain unanswered is where to source the content from. Even apps like Netflix could run out of new content soon. That means success in streaming may be offset by scarcity of new content. Will that be a new strain of the Corona virus in the entertainment industry?

All said and done, it will be all about streaming post-pandemic for entertainment platforms. And hanker after the money in viewers' wallets. Linear may be out to make room for on-demand services.

Create content and consolidate, stream content and survive. That could become the new vision statement for the entertainment industry players post-Corona.

4 Global Gaming Games

Already the gaming industry is global. Post Corona, this industry will scale new heights. Major beneficiaries of this coming explosion will be the established studios. For the smaller studios, this gaming groundburst will however turn out to be a moment of crisis post-Corona.

Productivity losses, difficult financing, looming recession, falling demand and slashed advertising revenues, well, their woes will be never-ending. They will also find it hard to get State support. So, the choice before them will be between shuttering down and selling out to larger players.

Given the fact gaming offers an array of options for safer connect, shared experiences, social distancing and societal intercourse, it will be natural that post-Corona gaming would turn into a much bigger global industry than we could have ever imagined.

Such is the power of esports, playing leagues will become prominent in our lives post-Corona. Leagues such as Overwatch and Call of Duty will become permanent fixtures in our online sports schedule.

Scan some vital statistics to realise how global is gaming now. With nearly 40 million gamers in the United Kingdom today, Britons are already spending 24 per cent more time on video games. Since the lockdown, global gaming has grown by 75 per cent.

On the flip side, as much as 35 per cent of the global population is spending more time playing video games now. Just sample this. Twitch alone notched up a staggering viewership of more than three billion hours during Corona-prompted lockdown. Incidentally, Twitch is operated by Twitch Interactive, a subsidiary of Amazon.

That means the global gaming industry is much larger than the global music industry and box office combined. People all over are not going to give up this addictive gaming routine so easily post-Corona. Top gaming companies like Tencent, Sony, Microsoft, Apple and Activision Blizzard, and their smorgasbords of innovatively flavoured gaming products, will become necessary indulgences for many.

Interesting to note here is the rising popularity of epsorts within the larger circle of the gaming industry. The example of F1 real-life drivers competing in Virtual Grand Prix competitions goes to prove that post-Corona gaming will become a must for large sections of global population.

In this gaming mania, global brands will jump in to tap the advertising potential of gaming. That would make the gaming industry much larger and truly global post-Corona. Then, gaming would have arrived as a new-found advertising alternative and would prove to be the turning point for in-game advertising.

The madness is not going to stop there. App developers will look at all these post-Corona developments as sexy opportunities for their own growth and popularity. According to Samuel Huber, CEO and co-founder of Admix, a monetisation platform for virtual reality and augmented reality based between London and San Francisco, playtimes will increase by about 20 per cent worldwide post-Corona.

That should be a major opportunity for global brands to reach more eyeballs. Gaming companies will view mobile games as the new social square where you can feel the real sense of society and community. With the need to game more thrown in. Will that be the new game post-Corona? Or, the new future version of Game of Thrones?

5 Colonisation of Social Lives

Will the social media turn more anti-social in the post-Corona world? That is one concern-filled poser people are lobbing at social scientists and media analysts. Social or anti-social, surely you will see a record-shattering usage of all social media platforms.

Record-shattering usage not only because more common-interest commentaries will be shared, not only because hot Corona-related news will be disseminated more and faster, not only because these platforms will double up as dependable lifelines of crisis information, not only because general concerns will be exchanged with greater frequency, but also because of greater misuse of social media with an eye on reaping rich political dividends.

Increasingly, post-Corona you will see social media platforms leveraged with greater lethal effect for demonstrating political one-upmanship, for propagating fake news, for staging Machiavellian manipulations, for posting conflict-triggering comments, for spreading sectarian viruses and for seeding communal hatred, among other devious purposes. Call that the new phenomenon of digital duplicity, colonisation of social lives, antisocialisation of classes and communities.

For instance, social media platforms might propagate Covid myths post-Corona, increasingly and intensively. The signs of that happening are already there. The American business magazine Forbes says as much as 12 per cent of the 1,000 surveyed people believed Corona was created by humans. That was clearly an after-effect of false social media propaganda.

Spread of such misinformation is right up the streets of social media platforms, a made-for-them opportunity. In a society badly wrecked by Covid-19, virus hoaxes and hastily-manufactured horror stories will find many takers post-Corona. If such hoaxes are going to be the reasons behind the coming surge in social media usage, that is not something to cheer about.

In democracies like India, social media will turn into a more handy tool for fake news and sensationalism. Some social media platforms in India even went to the extent of rehashing and re-serving a globally mispropagated rumour that it was a communal conspiracy to spread Corona nationwide. They were just blowing the trumpet of falsehood louder and louder to make fake news sound true.

Even more developed nations or faster-developing nations will not be far behind. We will see them unleashing a terror of intense toxicity characterised by war of words blaming opposition politicians, ghettoed communities and alien nationals, not only for any future viral spreads, but for anything that could go wrong.

This will take such nations to heights of political brinkmanship and diplomatic skulduggery, shattering global and national camaraderie into smithereens in the bargain.

In such a poison-filled atmosphere, thickened by toxic clouds unleashed by social media, wars will be fought tomorrow mostly on social media platforms, not on battlefields on the ground. Warmongers and hissy hatemongers will increasingly fall in love in large numbers with scheming social media platforms. Just because they are viral by nature.

Velocity will inspire veracity. The degree of virality will determine tomorrow whether a fake news item could easily pass the litmus test of truth. These prognoses should not sound like some prophesies of a modern-day Cassandra. The writing is already there, plastered all over the walls of sugary social media platforms.

6 Pathologial People-Anxiety

Wherever they are, the denizens of a post-pandemic planet will choose to remain socially distanced. Perhaps for a long time. Such self-enforced social distancing will precipitate an occupancy crisis leading to reduced revenues and cringed collections for bars, restaurants and all business entities that survive on packed houses.

All such businesses will struggle for recovery from the harsh after-effects of a pandemic that would have harmed the collective psyche of people, establishments and nations. Fear of surging crowds will see people-anxiety reach pathological levels resulting in lower footfalls in malls and smaller congregations in places of worship. That will be the new agoraphobia post-pandemic. And the new anthropophobia.

Despite the compulsions of social mourning, societies will turn resigned to the bitter reality of having to treat births and deaths, and all those birthday bashes, funerals, memorials, burials, weddings and receptions as private affairs with minimal crowding. Mourn in private will be the new narrative of post-demise scripts. Celebrate at home will be the new social paradigm.

There could be respite from milling crowds in usually-packed locations like public parks, beaches, lakes and riversides. Socially-distanced people will have to put up with spaced outdoor seatings in restaurants. Cosmetic, hairdressing and tanning salons will be asked to operate at half their capacity, with enforced physical distancing. That could turn most of them go into a mandated recession in their collections, leading to sellouts to larger chain salons.

Expect gyms to operate at 25 percent capacity, while showers and locker rooms may remain closed for the fear of contagion. Equipment will be disinfected after each use and customers will be asked to be hand-gloved all the time within gym premises.

Hybrid and vehicle ceremonies will be approved for graduations. But, outdoor ceremonies will remain distanced between family members and community groups.

Do not complain if you are asked to look inside eateries before entering. Number of people at beaches will be monitored. Number of people not wearing face masks will be penalised. Sports events and jamborees will have to follow social distancing norms. So, cities and local bodies might lose revenue across the board from sales tax to parking fees. That may result in many civic bodies going bankrupt and bust.

All areas, where people are most likely to get infected, like interactive stations at museums, will be monitored regularly. That might result in heartburns and even confrontations with managing authorities. Though physicians will be allowed to work, hospitals will be required to keep at least 25 per cent of their beds ready and reserved for any emergency or revisitation of infections.

Summer camps may remain unallowed for a long time. Movie theaters and restaurants will see a small bunch of slowly-returning customers, careful and cautious ever. This will leave these places of people-driven businesses struggling for recovery from the pains of a prolonged pandemic.

Surgeries may go elective. As far as prisons are concerned, they will have to follow social distancing norms. But, less-hardened convicts may be released, even before the end of their terms. Or, at the very least, allowed to go on bail or parole. This could result in spikes in the number of petty to moderately-serious crimes, causing greater headaches to already-stressed police force. Courts may prefer to hold video-enabled hearings, even long after Corona.

Domestic travel will be allowed in reduced frequencies and schools may remain encouraged to conduct their classes online. People may prefer to offer prayers within the comfort of their homes and religious festivals may turn out to be largely private affairs.

Online conferences will impact innovation. This will result in attendees putting up with reduced business opportunities. It would become difficult for marketing mavens to exchange best business practices over live-streamed summits.

Teleconferencing will become regular features in the calendar of many businessmen. Teleconferencing tools such as Microsoft Teams, Google Hangouts and Zoom will see a surge in their usage. That should lend an added push for 5G connectivity for home and office consumption. Reliable real time communication will become the lifeline for businesses, even for personal needs.

In-person events may slowly get phased out. Virtual conferences and webinars will become routine features in the diaries of businesses and business people. Because, as conference hosts, they will not only find virtual conferences easily scalable, flexible and manoeuvrable, but will also find them offering scope for greater control over the proceedings.

Evidences available so far hint at clients transforming into willing attendees of virtual events, never mind they are not high-profile occasions. For instance, the virtual exhibition platform V-Ex had more than 50,000 people visiting its online digital trade shows recently.

Surely, sooner or later, Internet goliaths including Facebook, Google and YouTube will fall head over heels in love with hosting virtual versions of their popular conferences. They may even form dedicated companies to launch their virtual-conference platforms for additional revenue streams. Or, acquire existing profitable virtual exhibition platforms.

Such a development will mine the immense potential of this virtual conference format. That could well be the bright dimension in a bleak post-pandemic geometry.

7 Teacher-Technology Online Optimisation

Imagine schools without students. Imagine students without classrooms. Imagine classrooms without lessons. This is not a scene from some offbeat docudrama. In fact, in all likelihood, this will be the new learning paradigm post-pandemic.

Imprisoned in an extended lockdown, school-going children are sure to forget the learning rigours and regimentation, the routine and the rote of a brick and mortar school. That memory loss will become a larger reality tomorrow thanks to adolescent video-game addiction, much of that developed during the lockdown days.

In this futuristic story, weak learners will become weaker, thus needing strong crutches of teaching and learning support. So, the post-pandemic education will be forced to turn into a combined contribution of initiators, instructors, subject specialists, learning advisers, career coaches, support staff and child psychologists. That will make education a holistic exercise in some sense of the term.

Spending much of their learning time at home before the watchful eyes of parents will make learners avoid wasteful distractions and stay on course. So, post-Corona, learners might lead a healthy and wholesome learning existence, thanks to the balanced intakes of knowledge, learning, entertainment and domestic togetherness.

That could result in their mental health getting shipshape, their learning aptitudes improving and their attitudes towards teachers altering for the good.

Overtime, post-Corona, vocational education will be seen as a must for kids by many parents. This will make vocational schools sought-after institutions post-crisis. In many homes, a broadband Internet connection or a WiFi-enabled laptops or smartphones will move up on the priority shopping list. In many welfare nations and nanny states, governments may step in to provide that WiFi connection and those gadgets free. When that happens, some serious learning will take place.

There is another bright spot in the post-pandemic education scene. That is technology complementing teachers, not replacing them. Such a complementary relationship between teachers and technology will usher in what should be called the teacher-technology online optimisation.

That is why usage of online teaching platforms is surging to giddying heights. This burst will prod educationists to do much soul-searching, resulting in the actualisation of that online optimisation.

A caveat here however. The innovation, the intelligent solutions and the insights that come with the teaching technologies will drive a sharp wedge between the illiterate poor and the literate rich. This wedge will get only deeper as education moves over to the online format lock, stock and barrel, sinking the poor into a deeper morass.

That seems a reality waiting to happen. Many schools in poor nations are scouting for temporary solutions for teaching to go on, but the quality of learning there is heavily impaired by the quality of digital technology on tap. Not just that, it is estimated that only around 60 per cent of the planet's population is online[1]. That adds to the woes of the illiterate and the technologically-challenged poor.

There is every possibility of homeschools becoming preferable options for young learners. With that, many states will recognise homeschooling as a perfectly legal alternative post-Covid. Such legalisation of homeschooling will provide legitimacy to homeschool co-operatives which will make online community-learning possible with conferencing technology tools, without having to worry about personal distancing.

Surely, homeschool cooperative[2]'s will offer an opportunity for learning from other parents with varied experiences and specialisations. More than that, these cooperatives will offer the socially-starved youngsters scope for much needed social intercourse. They may learn together. That itself will satisfy their hunger for social interactions.

---

1.   https://thenextweb.com/growth-quarters/2020/01/30/

        digital-trends-2020-every-single-stat-you-need-to-know-about-the-internet/

2.   https://en.wikipedia.org/wiki/Cooperative

Evidences are available to show homeschoolers have begun to discover the pleasures of leveraging Web 2.0[3] as a way to simulate homeschool cooperatives online. With active social networks[4], homeschoolers can discuss topics of common interest, chat on developing ideas, discuss threads in forums, share information and tips, and even participate in online classes through blackboard systems like the ones used by offline educational institutions.

Such an online homeschooling technology will provide interaction among the learners. Already, we are witnessing a surge in the usage of online education tech tools. Alphabet Inc's Google is marching ahead of its muscular competitors in education technology with a surge in the usage of its Google Classroom[5], a free service teachers use to send out assignments and communicate with learners.

Usage statistics on Google Classroom reveal it has doubled active users to more than 100 million since the beginning of March 2020. In turn, this surge is pushing other online Google educational products in the bargain. For instance, Google Meet, a videoconferencing app, is being used 25 times as much as it was in January 2020. And the broader G Suite for Education has 120 million users now in 2020, up from 90 million a year ago.

By the way, G Suite is a free-to-use learning management software. It is a suite of cloud computing, productivity tools and education software created by Google Cloud. This suite consists of Gmail, Google Hangouts, Google Calendar, Google Docs and the interactive white Jamboard, among others.

Thanks to the gradual spread of 5G technology, learners in many nations will learn anywhere anytime, in a wide range of easy-to-use formats. This format-adaptability will catch up with learners across the planet. Thereby the concept of digital education will itself go through a makeover to expand its online smorgasbord with a host of online learning experiences including live broadcasts.

As the online education mania becomes a contagion, public-private partnerships, the 3Ps as they are called, will take off in education. Particularly in developing economies.

3.	https://en.wikipedia.org/wiki/Web_2.0

4.	https://en.wikipedia.org/wiki/Social_networks

5.	https://www.hindustantimes.com/tech/
google-classroom-is-the-most-popular-education-app-on-play-store/story-ktgD4C4LLn0B24ZIbeLkaK.html

Learning consortiums and coalitions with diverse stakeholders including governments, publishers, education professionals, technology providers, and telecom network operators will happen. This should optimise the usage of online teacher-technology tools. When that happens, online education would not need to look back from its northward journey.

8 Exit Hot-Cross Bun Healthcare

Concerned and cautious, healthcare experts the world over are shedding sweat to ensure a repeat of the global covid contagion does not happen. That concern and caution will stimulate the ushering in of a new set of public health procedures and protocols, systems and setups.

From handling post-pandemic stress disorders intelligently to initiating new hygiene habits serially to putting through shifts in managing points of care decisively to offering healthcare plans suitably, healthcare should be changing for good.

Hospitals all over will be upgraded, will be equipped with better men and machines, will be strengthened by solid setups and sinewy systems, will be beefed up to handle complex patients and pathological conditions.

Handling emergency breakout situations will be the new focus of hospitals. Ensuring safer healthcare environment for patients will be their new priority. Overhauling intensive care systems will be their new emphasis.

Meanwhile, some countries have proposed that the detection of antibodies to the Corona virus SARS-CoV-2 could form the basis for what is called a pandemic passport. Such a risk-free certificate is supposed to enable ex-virus patients to travel, restart their usual routine and work in offices. These release certificates will be issued as smartphone Quick Response codes to those who are Covid-19 free.

Governments in Germany, Italy and Chile are among those toying with the idea of issuing such immunity passports. Other countries including United Kingdom will use permanently what is called the traffic light system to determine degrees of control on the basis of colour codes assigned to cities, districts and regions.

Hospitals of tomorrow will be expected to handle issuance of pandemic passports 24x7 after due diligence and due testing. Some national governments may even require their hospitals to manage surveillance and contact tracing to hunt down suspectedly symptomatic people.

Well, today all these are still in the realm of conjectures and guessworks. As questions pertaining to data protection, privacy violations, discriminatory practices and perverse incentives remain unanswered, hospitals are not yet clear about where they stand on this issue. However, answers or no answers, hospitals will be certainly required tomorrow to do more than clinical treatment of infected people.

Be that as it may, healthcare awareness programmes of States across the globe will place greater stress on personal and public hygiene practices such as regular handwashing. Social distancing measures and facemask-wearing practices will be in place permanently.

Tapping artificial intelligence algorithms in healthcare may soon become a healthcare imperative. These algorithms will be leveraged not only for sending early warnings of outbreaks, but also for testing Covid-19 suspects and the potentially infected. Hospitals will use artificial intelligence to manage their strained resources[1] optimally, accelerate the pace of research on contagion controls and get prepared better for the next healthcare crisis.

Digital health solutions will move centrestage in the fight against Corona. Telemedicine[2] and digital health technologies will be the new healthcare paradigms. Devices like digital stethoscopes, otoscopes and electrocardiogram monitors will move within common man's reach, to be used at home and anywhere, shifting the point-of-care to the patient. The results will be shared with doctors online. So, expect doctor-patient visits happening only when they are absolutely unavoidable and necessary.

In a post-pandemic world, telehealth options will expand beyond anybody's imagination. Fee-for-Service healthcare models will transform into value-based primary care. Increased use of technology will help slash high costs and inefficiencies in healthcare.

The traditional healthcare model of paying for every visit, paying after every consultation and paying for every hospital admission will be displaced gradually by monthly and yearly healthcare packages. This hot-cross bun healthcare, where you pay for every unit of the product, will bow out to let in healthcare packages that will be sold as mobile, basic, regular, standard and premium plans. That will be the Spotify moment or the Amazon Prime moment in healthcare.

---

1.   https://qventus.com/blog/predicting-the-effects-of-the-covid-pandemic-on-us-health-system-capacity/

2.   https://medicalfuturist.com/covid-19-was-needed-for-telemedicine-to-finally-go-mainstream/

Healthcare will then be sold more like mobile phone call-data packages offered by service providers. That will push out the fee-based healthcare business model to replace it with a subscription-based model. In the bargain, we will see the creation of a reliable healthcare infrastructure.

In such a trustworthy healthcare scenario, patient-care entities and organisations will develop a "co-operative healthcare info bank", wherein patient and pandemic data will be stored and shared, for discussions and analysis. Not only will such a bank equip hospitals to handle pandemic situations better, this info-bank concept will usher in a cohesively unique healthcare ecosystem that can rise up to any challenge.

Clues about the changing face of healthcare post-pandemic are already available in how the National Health Service is transforming. This publicly funded healthcare system in the United Kingdom, the largest single-payer healthcare system in the world, is collaborating with US technology companies such as Google of Alphabet Inc, Twitter, Facebook, Instagram, Microsoft and Amazon Web Services to create computer dashboards and front-end data platforms to fight pandemic outbreaks.

Such public-private partnerships will become the healthcare norm in many countries leading to the internationalistion of healthcare. Which will make possible global sharing of resources, expertise and information.

Meanwhile, the clinical staff of National Health Service are working in unrelated departments today. Even eye-nose-throat surgeons are said to be working in intensive care units and trauma care centres.

Such developments will become the norm worldwide and will bring about enduring shifts in the generalist-specialist equation. That will be the new healthcare paradigm, post-pandemic.

9 The Staycationisation Syndrome

Staycations. The post-pandemic planetarians will head towards them in a big way. Even years after the Corona virus vanishes without trace, let it be wishful thinking, denizens of this planet will recurringly have second thoughts about travelling afar.

It is precisely this mysophobia, the pathological fear of viruses and viral infections, that will keep holiday travellers away from alien destinations. What will they do then? Where will they go for pleasure? How will they spend their much longed-for holidays?

All valid questions. With a simple answer though. They will all turn to staycation options. They will explore a variety of choices to spend their holidays close to their homes in sanitized, self-contained and stand-alone private rental units including private villas that throw their doors open to local tourists and travellers.

Holidayers will toy with a host of proposals to revel in their hard-earned leisure in their home countries, away from nations that are hit hard by the pandemic. They will debate over an assemblage of ideas to celebrate their vacation in safe local attractions.

Surely, staycation resorts will spring up everywhere, near every tourist spot and near every holiday destination to satisfy people consumed by wanderlust. That way they can remain safe and at the same time get the feel of relaxing resorts. Many homes will double up as staycation resorts.

In these home resorts, fun-loving frolickers will turn creative and indulge in activities as diverse as hanging a hammock in their backyards, hosting fireside chats, dining alfresco, gardening creatively, adding swings to their balconies and giving the home a complete spring cleaning to cover everything from carpets to curtains and fans to floors, among many such sweaty and fat melting activities.

As home resorts and staycations pick up steam, travel hogs will travel to places nearer home and shift their allegiance to vacation rentals, dumping hotels in the bargain. Road trips will be preferred and air travel will be given the go-by.

People who own second houses and third houses will convert these properties into staycation homes that can be booked online and paid online using debit cards or credit cards. Why, there could be even staycation aggregators emerging in large numbers, a la Airbnb. Call that the Airbnb moment for the staycation industry.

This introvertisation of the travel industry should ground the hotel and airline companies badly, crashing their plans of occupancy and profit maximisation. In this process of painful transmogrification, the big gainers will be the peddlers of travel insurance and travel advisory products, all of them sold online. Travellers and short-distance tourists will never step out without proper travel insurance coverage.

Players like Airbnb and Marriott International will put through fundamental shifts in their business plans and revenue models. Domestic reservations and summer selling will become priority businesses for them.

Considering that the 93-year-old Marriott International is already suffering a 90 per cent drop in its China business post-pandemic, such a shift will become inevitable across the board. This will benefit domestic and summer travellers, who will enjoy heavily discounted rates.

The recent Travel Sentiment Study-Wave 7 on American travellers done by the Ohio-based market research consultancy Longwoods International in collaboration with the Florida-based travel solutions company Miles Partnership shows that 82 per cent of them changed their travel plans for the next six months. Of these, 50 percent have said they will cancel their trips and 45 per cent said they will reduce travel in the next six months.

Such a demand-dip will force the aviation industry to slash airfares, adjust their cancellation policies and accommodate their changing plans. Even vacation rentals will usher in a very flexible and friendly cancellation rules. Tomorrow, post-pandemic, the travellers will even determine the rates. Call it the pay-as-you-please tariff model.

This pay-whatever-you-feel-like model that can be found in restaurants like Lentil At Anything in Melbourne, Soul Kitchen in New Jersey, Ziferblat in London and De Culinaire Werkplatts in Amsterdam will spread its tentacles in the aviation and staycation industry too. More in the restaurant network tomorrow. Such donation-driven staycation homes and restaurants will restore supply chains in the travel and tourism industry over the long haul.

Meanwhile, the MICE tourism industry that encompasses meetings, incentives, conferences and exhibitions too will embrace this model. With the promise of a Pandemic-unfriendly seating arrangements thrown in.

This post-pandemic makeover however will hit hard the economies that rely heavily on tourism. These economies will get busy putting in place sweeping staycation reforms and staycation infrastructure to cushion their losses. That is why you will see, in all likelihood, a post-pandemic acceleration in the staycationisation process.

10 Digital Taxes and Deglobalisation

As the euphemistic developing nations of the world are pushed to the margins of a fractious global digital tax system, global tax negotiations will change tack post-pandemic. To begin with, that course-corrective action will change globally accepted formats of fiscal discussion.

Global tax negotiations and discussions will happen over more empowering teleconferences, appealing video telephony platforms and streaming video conferences. In-person meetings will be shunned and global taxation may begin to turn inwards. That will bring about breezy changes in the equation between the developing and the developed world, ultimately altering the contours of global digital taxation.

Such an overhauling change will see Europe and the American subcontinent discovering the pleasures of agreement and acceptance, peaceful co-existence and comity with the rest of the world. So, who knows, in all probability, the high-profile transatlantic disagreement may give way to a cohesive unification of ideals. Not only among the Pan-European nations, not only within OECD nations, among the more disadvantaged developing nations as well.

In the process, the focus of global fiscal discussions and debates will shift from short-term politico-economic expediencies to long-term global consensus and cooperation. Under the canopy of these shifts, a novel brand of fiscal politics will emerge to threaten the very survival of authoritarian and oligarchic formations such as OECD. That may set the ball of deglobalisation rolling.

As global tax consensus will be the new global fiscal paradigm, digital tax negotiations will get deglobalised. That will give rise to a new digital tax domain that will be of great interest to regional politicians, who may begin slashing investments in digital projects. Of course, as a result, global tax negotiations may be delayed for ever. Even pushed back, setting the post-pandemic deglobalisation on fire.

All these changes will cast their nets far and wide, affecting all countries, large and small, in varying degrees. The developing countries will be particularly slammed in a big way. Not only will they be unable to handle their domestic imperatives, they will also find it difficult to come to terms with the new global tax negotiation compulsions. That is where global tax discussions will get shallower and shallower, more fragmented and more fragile.

There is a plus-sign appearing visibly bright in this dismal sky. The increased move towards videoconferences will reduce participation costs, travel expenses and time investments. In turn, this will see non-OECD nations emerging stronger with greater participatory roles in the new world order. With personal interactions falling to the minimum, new centres of authority may emerge in the form of regional groupings, not only in Europe and the American subcontinent, elsewhere too. Along with that new clusters of regional bargaining power will be birthed.

All these shakes and jolts will force governments to shift their focus in digital tax negotiations. Against the backdrop of a changed politico-economic landscape, nations will mobilise their tax systems to tackle the economic crisis that will blow up on their faces, placing pressure on national fiscal capacity. Alongside, nations will encourage digital business organisations to contribute more to the national exchequer as they will see their profits rising. There may be a temptation to tax digital service companies more. Will that prove to be the killing the golden duck that lays golden eggs?

The post-pandemic global downturn will hit developing economies harder, in turn forcing governments to look at corporations as milch cows and begin raising corporate taxes in general, digital economy taxes in particular. That is sure to create an environment where individual personal taxes will be heavily cross-subsidised by steeply rising corporate taxes and bulging levies on digital corporations.

In the process, developing nations may discover their cloaked identities and muffled voices in the global fora. They may bring back capital controls and restrictions on multinational company investments, signalling their turn inwards and making globalisation retreat further.

Meanwhile, many European countries will come down harshly on digital corporations and impose stiff taxes on their profits. Why, United Kingdom is already eyeing opportunities to tax the UK revenues of American tech giants. Quite natural that USA is viewing digital taxes as direct attack on its interests and this may result in retaliation with tariffs on European imports. So much for global cooperation.

Where will all these lead to? We may see taxation of the digital economy emerging post-pandemic to be a major bone of contention between the developed world and the developing world. Most developed nations will rise up to the challenge and begin biting the bullet by repealing digital services tax on their companies. But, in developing economies, digital taxes will become willy nilly the hottest issue, burning and raging.

Populist governments in such developing economies will begin redistributing profits of digital companies to fund their public infrastructure projects, poverty alleviation schemes and social welfare plans. Why, even to fund redemption of their massive debt piles. That is when globalisation would have taken a decisive step backward.

11 Universalisation of Introvertism

Introvertism and isolationism. Seclusionism and self-reliance. As these words turn into highfalutin jargons and blurred fuzzwords in the post-pandemic years, they will enter the vocabulary of even laymen across nations.

One thing for sure, however. The speed and the spread of the digital economy will squeeze the world deeper into its many hunkered crevices, forcing this planet to withdraw itself into a Coronaphobic shell and placing a premium on introvertism. In the process, pushing internationalism to the backburner.

This phenomenon of turning inwards will shape nations, will mould their political philosophies, will define their economic policies and will recolour their external affairs post-pandemic. The unifying concept of globalisation will slowly give way to the birth of many self-reliant states.

Inevitably, over the long haul, this universal introvertism will perpetuate sea changes in coercion-employing territorial states, in politico-cultural nation states and in the singular canopy of globalisation. Also in the superpowers-influenced world economic order, in the ever-delicate global diplomatic ties, in the forever-volatile global military relations, in the undefined national interests, in the bubbly social life, in the pulsating global supply chains and in the fluid world trade connections, among others.

Many nations will shift their emphasis to self reliance, moving away from globalisation. Capital controls may come back and stock markets may be closed for aliens. International travel will be viewed with suspicion.

Slowly but surely, global corporations will move down the list of governmental and consumer preferences. Trade wars will become the new normal in global trade. All these when global unity, global peace and global coexistence will be the need of the hour. In itself, such an inclination to look inward will carry within itself the seeds of conflicts of interest and clashes of ideology.

Challenges such as socio-economic inequalities are already posing a threat to the very survival of the concept of an European Union, a federation of territorial states in a manner of speaking. Buffeted by Brexit, the already gasping European Union will now see, post-pandemic, the process of deplorable desynergisation of its plans hastened.

Meanwhile, ethnically diverse and culturally autonomous nation states, of course many of them, will not be able to resist the temptation of turning into ethnically-cleansed autocracies and theocracies, citing the pandemic as an excuse. India could be a classic example of this phenomenon as the numerically-strong Hindu nationalists will go about blaming a section of the non-Hindus for everything that will go wrong, and in the process, try hard to isolate the latter from the mainstream.

In most of these nation states, secessionist warfare will don new colours by enabling non-State actors gain control over everything from religious zealotry to separatist propaganda. Proxy wars will intensify in the process. State terrorism will turn into instruments of foreign policy, to be exploited by non-State actors, to be used against adversaries.

Signs of these turning into a reality are already visible in some nation states where terror entities like the Islamic State of Iraq and the Levant, Taliban, Al-Qaeeda and Lashkar-e-Taiba are attempting to impose theocracies or autocracies. In self-determination-seeking nation states like the People's Republic of China-controlled Hong Kong and the Israel-controlled Gaza, West Bank and East Jerusalem, we may see a resurgence of nationalism.

As controlling governments divert their resources for the prevention of another pandemic, these nation states will have a field day, with no one to frustrate their attempts to gain supremacy. That will put finishing touches on the paint-fresh portraits of universalised introvertism and isolationism.

12 Europe's Phoenix Moment

As if the bleak prospect of introvertism and isolationism turning nations and governments, companies and corporations, institutions and individuals into inward-looking bundles is not enough, a new world order threatens to emerge post-Corona. The causative factors behind the creation of that new world order are many. Some of them are already manifesting themselves in different directions.

The spat between USA and China threatens to rise to a crescendo and will go on to deepen the divide, tearing the existing world trade order. The credibility of the United Nations and its specialised agencies, already headed south, would have finally scraped the bottom.

Emboldened by the widespread post-Covid passivity and nervousness, autocratic and dissent-hating governments will be violating civil liberties more frequently and more intensely. Above all, an expansionist China will use this pandemic-triggered panic as an opportune time for aggressive territorial incursions in a bid to extend its political hegemony far and wide.

If these symptoms do not announce the arrival of the new world order, what will? In that new world order, authoritarian China will be seen as a failed global super power aspirant. That will be largely because the post-pandemic planet is sure to view aggression-loving China as a metaphor for misinformation and manipulation.

History has always demonstrated that nations capable of leading others are those capable of solving global problems, providing a decisive leadership and offering a direction for the future. In that respect, America was a leader post-war.

That role may be usurped by a more potent Europe tomorrow. Or by a powerful group of handpicked European nations. All global eyes will then focus on Europe. After the Nazism of Hitler and the Fascism of Mussolini, it will be the first-ever show of dominance by Europe.

In this new world order where Europe will call the shots, European nations will jostle for a front seat using nationalism, a la Hitler. They will soon discover that nationalism is not going to work for them in the long run.

Sooner or later they will realise that by cooperating they can handle future pandemics better, can generate workable pandemic responses, can produce superior pandemic solutions and can address climate change issues decisively. That realisation will push all those nationalism-mouthing empty jingoists behind.

Sure, post-pandemic, every nation will look inward, will focus on being self-reliant and self-dependent. But, it will be a slippery ground for the European nations as they struggle to strike the right balance between forced nationalism and peaceful co-existence, between self-dependence and mutual cooperation. Striking that balance will be more difficult than the ordeal of spending the pandemic years in suspense.

In this suspense-filled environment, right-wing politics may try to dig deep into the shifting sands of politico-nation marketplaces. In that process, nationalists could try to marginalise globalists. But, these nationalists will eventually discover to their dismay that only solidarity can push America and China back. That solidarity will induce Europe to act in the larger interests of its co-operating nationalistic governments.

The world may then sit up, take notice of Europe's rise and go on to brand this phenomenon as Europe's Phoenix Moment. With such close cooperation, European nations will be able to build workable healthcare systems and even share Covid vaccine patents. The model of National Health System may be replicated across Europe.

In its Phoenix moment, Europe may usher in a new brand of governance and make the European Union, whatever loose structure it takes, more resilient. Despite that resilience, some member nations may continue to close their markets to the outside world in a bid to magnify the role of the state in their inward-looking economies. That will put Europe's democratic systems through a litmus test. Perhaps a trial by fire by competing populists, authoritarians and democrats.

Populists may continue to heap pandemic insults on foreigners, justify their aversion to open immigration and turn more inward. Authoritarians may tighten their grips on their hapless states in the name of appropriate pandemic responses. In the ensuing pandemonium, Europe will eventually realise only democracy works best even in times of pandemic crisis. That is why a renewed solidarity among European nations is a big possibility.

The members of European Union will leverage this solidarity to keep China at bay. It will be little surprising if they decide to come together as a confederation, perhaps loose and informal, to self-regulate their producers, marketeers and exporters. And to build just-in-time supply chain alternatives to whittle down dependence on China. They may even stand by each other to fight climate change.

Going by that futuristic yardstick, Europe may steal a march over United States and China. Can that be called the Covidisation of the New European Union?

13 The Oxymoronic Trade Order

Common markets that are inward-looking. Unions of states that are introverted. Comity of nations that are controlled. Democracies that are authoritarian. Federations that are fragmented. Agreed, all opulent oxymorons. Nevertheless. Look not far.

In a post-pandemic milieu, a new world trade order must be nigh. How about a Brazil-centric Latin American Union or an India-centric Asian Union or a Franco-German-centric European Union? Sure, such state centricities will not be alien to post-pandemic trade blocs.

These trade formations will debate heatedly the role of China in international trade in the coming years. They may even come to the point of boycotting Chinese imports. From there on, they may move ahead to build import-substituting capacities and just-in-time supply chains in their common market areas. Until that fructifies in full measure, restricted Chinese imports may be permitted, albeit with high tariff.

As the internecine trade war tears into America and China, spats between them will reach a new crescendo. America will impose more strangulating tariffs on Chinese imports and will explore options to move production to local manufacturing units. It has already withdrawn itself from the Transatlantic Trade and Investment Partnership, the ongoing talks with the European Union notwithstanding.

All these provide foretaste of the coming new trade regime, a new world trade order and a new world financial order, in a manner of speaking. Territorial trade blocs may emerge to protect the interests of territorial states like Scandinavia, South East Asia and Central Europe. Even the Indian subcontinent may join the list of such aspiring territorial states.

China's global supply chains will snap to let in economies of Japan, South Korea and India, which all have the wherewithal to build global supply alternatives. These three nations may leverage their untapped potential to emerge as the new supply-chain czars and fill in the vacuum. Why, they could even form a trade alliance. Brazil, Russia and South Africa may also be the hopefuls to join that race.

The overriding consideration for creating such trade blocs will be to skirt around pandemic-triggered situations in a bid to ensure supply chains are up and delivering. Another consideration will be to create strategic supply-clusters that can be switched on and off at will.

This desperation to create standby supply hubs and substituting supply chains will ensure relocation of manufacturing closer to the markets, never mind the cost factor. Shorter supply chains will also help combat climate change. That is a bonus.

Many nations are already exploring options to shift their production facilities and companies away from China. Japan is one of them. In the process, the silo mentality, call it the silo thinking or the silo vision, will be abandoned. The inward-looking mindset that prevents nations from sharing information and resources with other members of the same common market will give way to strategic trade zone partnerships.

In that respect, do not be surprised if an African Common Market or a Latin American Common market or an Australian Common Market begins to take shape post-pandemic. Preventing overdependence on one predominant supply chain will become the priority before the members and partners of any common market.

Mechanisms will be put in place to insulate against opportunistic Chinese entities hunting for bargains in the corporate control market. Efforts will be put through to reduce dependencies in technology imports from China. Accelerated investments will make way into futuristic technologies such as artificial intelligence. Surveillance will be stepped up against suspicious offshore economic activities.

Post-pandemic, economic nationalism will be there on the lips of the heads of every nation. Most nation-states will embrace domestic production policies to meet their needs. To make that happen, these nation-states will precipitate dilution of Chinese control on global supply chains. All in a bid to put the new world order firmly in its place.

Putting the best foot forward, nation-states will do everything to check total collapse of their economies. Relief measures, recovery plans and revival strategies will be kicked off in right earnest in each of these economies. However, some of these plans may conflict with the overall goals of the common market. Nevertheless.

Such inherent conflicts, like the east-west and the north-south disagreements, may worsen in post-Covid days. That may threaten the very survival of the common markets. Not to despair. It will all end up in the creation of many smaller common market zones in continents. That will be the post-pandemic planet's Balkan Moment.

14 Exit Marshalls and Molotovs

If the World Health Organization is to be believed, the catastrophic waves of the Corona pandemic would never abate. That will surely make the coming global depression the longest one in living memory.

The looming depression will break the backs of global supply chains, setting in motion dramatic changes in the world financial order. Banking systems will crumble, financial players will go broke, the US dollar will decline and monetary funds will dissolve into inaction. One cannot imagine the sheer spread of the resulting monetary jungle, a gory metaphor for monetary lawlessness.

Even crypto-currencies will not be able to salvage the crumbling world financial order. Everywhere, governments will be seen clamouring for debt-cancellations, moratoriums and monetary relief packages from their central banks.

All these gloomy prognoses about the impending financial doom should make you believe the Cassandra for a change. If she is to be trusted, it may become difficult for the American Dollar to continue for long as the world's reserve currency. At the very least, the pre-eminence of American dollar in the global monetary system will become questionable and debatable.

Even banks outside America will, sooner or later, look at offshore dollar creations, through issuance of dollar-denominated loans, with suspicion. Add to this the menace of shadow banks spinning innovative instruments of finance, the decline of the Dollar would be somewhat complete.

Finance policies will be self-centred, like all other sectors in global economies. Inward-looking states and central banks will mould with alacrity equally inward-looking monetary policies. Corporate entities will be encouraged to invest locally. As a result, an irrational phobia of multinational companies will spread through the system. These shocks will begin to chisel the new world financial order.

Such a new world financial order will pivot on how soon Eastern-South Eastern Asia and Europe rise to the occasion. Nation-states like Japan, South Korea, France and Germany, and city-states like Singapore will call the shots in the new world financial order.

Autonomous special administrative regions like Hong Kong, which are offshore financial centres, will see the spirit of nationalism soar. This will enable Hong Kong to snap the Chinese umbilical cord and morph into a major financial destination for global investments. Be that as it may, finally the economies that are able to manage both the supply and the demand sides of their economies, efficiently and democratically, will decide the contours and colours of the new world financial order.

In that new world financial order where companies go bust regularly, governments will set aside governance to manage serial relief programmes. These programmes may not work the way they should. With that the state-owned banks will play second fiddles to shadow banks that spin shadow finance.

Shadow banks are not absolutely immune to infections inflicted by pandemics like Covid. They are the first to fall during moments of crisis. That will certainly happen now post-Corona, triggering a cascading failure in the overall financial order. Political upheavals, if any, in infected economies will make the cascade widespread.

Every crisis comes with its own opportunities. Post-Covid, that opportunity may arrive in various avatars. Monetary blocs, a la trade blocs, will be the most significant of them. As those monetary blocs vie with each other for the global financial cake, there will be demands for protection of monetary rights and privileges.

Precisely these vociferous demands will midwife a new global financial generation marked by an international monetary federation. If such a federation is formed, it may experience recurrent ulcerating conflicts with the International Monetary Fund, throwing the world financial order into a vortex of long turmoil and turbulence. That will see a whole lot of banks going bust in the process.

Such an unmitigated turbulence will prevent the global biggies, particularly America and China, from being significant players. Not just that. The turbulence will leave the global biggies, their governments, their ruling political dispensations and their pompous heads of states more muddled, with their financial and monetary visions sinking into a thick haze.

Will this financial upheaval turn into a moment of reckoning for Europe? Will bank busts in biggie economies offer Europe enough time to emerge as the architects of the new world financial order? They will, only if Europe gets its act together by chaperoning the reforms that are waiting in the wings.

In that Europe-centric new world financial order, shadow banks are likely to be regulated to ensure shadow finance gets gradually eclipsed by a globalised Euro. That monetary globalisation should then accelerate the creation of monetary blocs in the world. There could be a dominant Euro Bloc, with the Dollar Bloc and the Renminbi Bloc tiptoeing behind.

That could well turn out to be a eureka moment for the European Monetary Union. From there on, this European Monetary Union may move ahead to double up as an able alternative to the US Federal Reserve or the Bank of England or the People's Bank of China. It can very well then prove to be the guardian angel for dark continents. Also for Covid-hit regions needing monetary support via new credit lines.

Such role enhancements and functional enrichments of the European Monetary Union will enable Europe to rally under the Union's banner. Rally for what? To bring together its constituent nations and leverage that togetherness to blast the obstacles that are blocking European unity. What a sunrise moment that would be for Europe!

Finally, the Marshalls will be out. The Molotovs will be out. The Comecons will be out. The Merkels will be in. Effective handling of all pandemics, epidemiological and financial, will be in. That will be the beginning of a new Europe-centric world financial order.

15 The New World Health Order

If the pandemic brings in its wake a reworked geopolitical order, a redrawn world trade order and a reshaped global financial order, can a new world health order be far behind?

Sculpted by nations that steal a lead in global healthcare, the new world health order will be determined largely by the combined might of their healthcare patents, their innovative healthcare solutions and by their robust medical research.

Not very long ago, the world order was dictated largely by the capitalists and the protagonists of the industrial revolution. Tomorrow it will be outlined by nations that offer universal healthcare technology solutions and make the 194 member-strong World Health Organisation democratic and superpower-neutral.

Will healthcare technology leaders become parts of the new Allies in the post-pandemic scenario? Will the pandemic rogue China and its cohorts like North Korea and Pakistan constitute the new Axis? The colour and the complexion of the new world health order will be largely influenced by nations that are able to churn out positive pandemic responses and solutions on a continuing basis, crisis or no crisis.

Who are these gifted and godly nations? First of all, they can be identified from their ever-alert, swiftly-acting and proactive public healthcare authorities who support a wide network of well-oiled private healthcare providers. Make no mistake, the size will not matter, it is the swiftness that will matter in the new world health order tomorrow.

The first hammer hit will land when healthcare states will actively begin exploring alternative sources of medical supplies. New supply chains will be formed for sourcing bulk drugs, drug ancillaries, antibiotics, supplements and personal protective equipment.

Uppermost in the minds of healthcare states will be the creation of strategic reserves of vital medical products and disruption-proof supplies. Signs of that happening are already blinking with the launch of the European RescEU programme for generating round-the-year pandemic responses and for whittling down overdependence on a single-supply source like China. From there on, healthcare states will move ahead to bring together their resources to fight supply chain tyrannies.

Succinctly speaking, nation states that make vaccine breakthroughs, make rigorous testing and contact tracing their permanent healthcare missions and take decisive steps in bringing global healthcare solidarity will be seen as potential leaders in the new world health order.

Sure, post-Covid, potential global healthcare leaders may go ahead to make their central banks more autonomous and depoliticised. Central banks of these leaders may be equipped with greater authority to tap the synergies between the matrix of proactive monetary policies, democratic relief packages and just-in-time pandemic controls.

What a good pandemic management means is this. Manage the pandemic efficiently, transparently and democratically. Share healthcare patents impartially. Generate effective pandemic-prevention responses continually. Build post-pandemic healthcare grids to shelter the underprivileged. It is such a management that will decide who is who in the new world health order.

Seismic changes will rock the World Health Organisation in the post-pandemic years, perhaps altering world health order equations. The symptoms are already showing up. America is withdrawing aid to the World Health Organisation. More, India has been elected to the Chair of the Organisation's Executive Board. Australia is demanding an inquiry into the Covid crisis. In the days to come after Corona, isolation of China in the world health order will only increase.

Will that isolation become long lasting? That depends on how soon the Organisation is able to make its planning less closed, make its budgets reflect ground realities in healthcare and make its activities more transparent and tangible. It will also depend on how willingly member countries throw their treasury chests open for mandatory assessments and for meeting the Organisation's emaciated healthcare budgets.

When member countries rise up to such challenges, it will mark the beginning of an era of attitudinal changes in the Organisation. In turn, these attitudinal changes could see the clouds of global healthcare consensus and cooperation forming over time.

In quest of such a healthcare consensus, member nations may demand the Organisation's headquarters be shifted from Geneva to somewhere in sub-Saharan Africa. They may also be convinced that the Organisation can address global healthcare priorities better if it reorganises itself into smaller territorial groups focussed on regions vulnerable to heightened pandemic threats.

Territorial reorganisation will not be enough. The Organisation should use Covid as a reference point for moving away from China and letting in Taiwan as a full-fledged member. If all the non-aligned members clamour for making the Organisation apolitical, democratic, and less beholden to aid-extending superpowers, that may be the beginning of the new world health order.

In such a scenario, the Organisation would be less susceptible to manipulation by a single superpower member. By assuring financial aid after America's threat, China is attempting to annex the World Health Organisation into its hegemony. Capture the Organisation, that is what it boils down to.

When that attempt is foiled by the collective determination of healthcare democrats across the planet, a new world health order is bound to emerge. The colour of that new world health order will depend ultimately on who is the victor and who is the vanquished in the now all-consuming Covid battle.

16 The Damoclean Privacy Sword

The pandemic is fast piercing the mask of safety and security private healthcare data wears. In the bargain, it is exposing the ugly faces of data-gathering apps and social media channels, raising privacy concerns. Definitely, data privacy will become a matter of grave concern post-pandemic.

As tech-medico interplays intensify across the planet, digital volumes of healthcare data should surge exponentially post-Covid. Much of the public healthcare data is freely available, accessible and shareable. However, tech giants hold monopolistic controls over sets of private data, all related to their users, their locations and their contacts, among others.

It is very unlikely that these tech players will open up their private data chests for contact tracing and corona tracking. That is when they will be at loggerheads with governments. Extracting that private data from the tech giants will be a Minotaurean task, nearly impossible.

At the same time, it cannot be said with certainty that the private data-possessing tech titans will not sell such personal information and data to market research organisations, covetous corporates, tracking and tracing entities and manipulating governments. Where does that leave you all?

Data users, both corporates and individuals, will raise their clamouring voices for making their personal data secure. Despite unanimity on this issue, despite holy pronouncements by courts and governments, grey areas will remain.

After all, it is in the interest of authoritarian governments that data protection remains flexional. Only such fluidity will offer the needed loophole for mercenary private healthcare providers to hawk the data in their possession to paying info vultures. The unsavoury Facebook-Cambridge Analytica scandal is still fresh in our collective memories. Prior to that, Google's Google Flu was the target of privacy activists. Nothing has been since then to address data privacy issues.

Social media players and search engines may thump their chests and boast of having launched anonymised data. But, that will not work, what with the absence of clear rules for anonymization and making data secure. Google Flu Trends may be an effective tracking data, but what use when these rules seem to be far off. Muddle headedness will be the norm when it comes to making data privacy a reality.

Medical records will be increasingly digitised by Covid hospitals, which are generally run by governments. Patients and their families trust these hospitals when they fill out forms with personal details and demographic data. That trust could be breached anytime as public healthcare outfits become easy preys to marauding marketeers and manipulative politicians.

This data privacy concern may force data democrats and privacy champions to demand to put in place an autonomous constitutional authority responsible for data privacy governance. Such an authority may not only be trusted with user data, will also function as data privacy watchdog. Will that authority see the light of the day with app autocracy and tech tyranny looming largely over us?

There is another danger we face in the post-pandemic environment. Dissent-intolerant governments will be tempted to set aside privacy laws in the name of Covid emergency. These governments will certainly bring in surveillance programmes that will define the contours of their controlled democracies.

Why special surveillance programmes? United Kingdom's contact-tracing app from its National Health Service may well do that job tomorrow. India's contact-tracing mobile app Aarogya Setu may permanently track all the employees in its economy for reasons other than Corona. Singapore's Bluetooth-based TraceTogether app may be used for ever to generate false alarms for ulterior motives. Iran is doing all that already with its contact-tracing apps.

Sure, privacy concerns will surge in the post-Corona world with the 40-odd contact-tracing apps around the planet and more in the works. For instance, the satellite-based Global positioning system, largely used by contact-tracing apps, can facilitate surveillance and carry out mobile phone espionage. Shockingly, most of them do not have any privacy policy worth the name.

China provides a foretaste of privacy violations that could assail its citizens in a post-pandemic scenario. The dragon is curtailing freedom of its denizens to move by using their own mobile handsets. More, it is using their digital payment data to track their shopping expeditions. All of these have the nasty habit of staying permanently in the rule books.

The coming scenario post-Covid is simple to understand. Privacy-violating and data-thirsting governments will run amok to trample democracy, perhaps using equally culpable corporates as instruments of complicity. What use contact-tracing without capacity-testing?

Perhaps there is. Ask the lockdown-thirsting leaders. Ask the data-hungry demons. Ask the dissent-hating dictators. Ask the tracking and tracing tyrants. You can then hear the disheartening post-pandemic story of Data Privacy.

17 The World Narrow Web

Populists and propagandists are control freaks. They know a pandemic is a perfect setting for playing their games of curbing and closing, dividing and delinking. See them already hoisted on to the World Wide Web, attempting to clip the global wings of internet.

Some have already done that job. Some will finish that job tomorrow post-pandemic. One thing for sure. The actions and inactions of populists and propagandists will certainly make the internet more introverted and more inward-looking, more parochial and more partisan.

These populists and propagandists are not going to bother about the internet turning into a non-caring non-entity when it comes to societal welfare. That is the real danger tomorrow, pandemic or no pandemic.

As the internet turns antisocial in a manner of speaking, the whole bunch of authoritarians, autocrats, dictators, dissent-haters and tyrants will pummel the global internet network and the World Wide Web into submission to serve their partisan ends and political agendas. Tomorrow, that will be a cause for grave concern for privacy advocates as well.

Despite privacy concerns, internet will continue to be as oligarchic as ever. Nonchalant, internet giants will only go on to tighten their grips around the world wide web. In the process, making the web more centralised and concentrated.

That is why our fear of internet oligarchists is real. In all likelihood, these oligarchists will spread their influence far and wide on the world wide web to erect barriers on the information sharing highway. They will continue to aggregate personal information of users and exploit them to expand their information hegemony and marketing dominance, besides bolstering their bottomlines. When push comes to shove, inventors and innovators will finally exit the internet space.

As if all these were not enough, authoritarian governments will go extra lengths to up the ante in this contest for control over the internet. Thirsting for information and hungering for authority, they will surely carve out their national webs, balkanising the internet further.

Such walled and closed-door garden networks will go about merrily controlling, regulating, managing and monitoring the info-accessing and info-sharing habits of its denizens. China has carved out such a national internet already. It is public knowledge that China's Great Firewall controls information and data filtering into that country.

Islamic countries like Iran are known to have such a closed fundamentalist halal internet for some time now. Why, North Korea's two-decade old Kwangmyong internet network belongs to that category of closed internet spaces. Cuba and Myanmar too have similar closed internets.

Tomorrow, India may have a similar walled internet that would conform to Hindutva values. Localized email and search engine services will be generously thrown in to bring all the Hindus in India together.

Russia has already begun patrolling its internet and exploring ways for erecting a digital border wall. Why, Indonesia too is about to launch its version of national internet, which in all likelihood will be a closed affair. Pakistan may follow suit. All of them violating the open spirit of the internet with impunity. Now on, all these closed and shut strategies will be in the name of the pandemic.

The numbers of such internet-introvert nations will continue to grow further along with cases of Corona infections. The tribe of internet deciders, which includes India, Israel, Brazil and Singapore, may influence the future of the internet. That will not make much of a difference.

As national internets spring up elsewhere post pandemic, access to foreign media will be restricted, partisan national internet alternatives will be propped up and coloured propaganda will be unleashed on closed web spaces. All in the name of controlling the pandemic, keeping a tab on its spread and checking its devastating creep.

By the way, this process of carving national internets, making the internet exist in pieces within several national borders, will shut the open internet. Worse, this process will transform internet governance into a propagandistic affair and will reduce the internet to a handmaiden of authoritarian governments.

The result will be unpalatable to most of us. Malawares and misinformation, fake news and falsehood will become the cherished goals of national internets.

At the same time, regions like America may have dual internets post-pandemic. That is, an open internet for the home region and a closed internet for the rest of the world. Tech players like Alphabet and Microsoft may chip in to make the American dual internet a reality. That will sound the death knell for the Tim Berners-Lee's dream of a democratic World Wide Web and an egalitarian internet.

Sadly, the growing introvertism of the internet and the parochialism of the World Wide Web is evident everywhere now, and bound to grow further post-Corona. The introvertism and parochialism appears to run so deep in the collective psyche of nation-states that it will not go away.

On the contrary, more countries will prefer to lead duplicitous digital lives. Why, countries like Zimbabwe, Myanmar, Brazil, China and Mexico may permanently have their internets of denial attempting to conceal more Covid info than what they reveal.

Elsewhere in the United Kingdom and India, websites are already knee-deep into anti-muslim propaganda blaming the minority community for the Corona spread. This minority-hate will be fuelled further by national internets tomorrow.

Well, China and Egypt will throw scribes behind bars for speaking on Covid. Assaults on media and media freedom will rise. Partisan attitudes, like the ones on display in Rohingya refugee camps in Bangladesh, will harden. In Kashmir, the dissent-hating government may order that the internet moves slower, preventing healthcare workers and supplies from streaming in. Islamic nation-states may blacklist WhatsApp and Skype permanently, all in the name of curbing panic news spreads.

Certainly, all these instances digital duplicity do offer an acidic foretaste of things to come. In all probability, the World Wide Web will become narrower with a swarm of internet bans and restrictions, shutdowns and subversions by authoritarian regimes trying to throttle it. Will that make it the World Narrow Web?

18 Ominous Localisation Overhang

Thanks to Edward Snowden, data localisation got the push after 2013. Today, national internets are prodding nations to move towards greater degrees of data localisation. Post-pandemic, these data localisation attempts will only increase and intensify.

As the devastating pandemic turns the planet inward-looking, many nations will openly profess to regulate citizens' data using localisation rules. These nations may say that data localisation is for accelerating their economies. In fact, what they have in mind is surveillance of their own citizens.

Forget the economies of geographical aggregation of data, expect the power-hungry politicians to make moves to store all the data locally and make overseas data transfer difficult. That is why data localisation rules are multiplying at an alarming rate. Worse, they will multiply at a greater rate post pandemic, diverting internet traffic to numerous national channels.

Through the thicket of such protectionist data localisation rules, governments will try increasingly to store citizens' data within their borders. All these governments will see to it that data cannot be transferred unless they meet local privacy or data protection laws and unless they are satisfied about how the information will be used.

Where will this lead to? Restrictive data residency laws will spring up in many geographies. Curb-happy governments will ensure collection and processing of data happen within their national boundaries, and obliterated from alien systems. Already, China localises all personal, business and financial data of her citizens. Russia too does that. Countries like Indonesia and India may join this comprehensive data localising club tomorrow.

As more countries localise data, the concept of data sovereignty will catch on. The rise of cloud computing will only prod many countries to enact watertight laws for controlling and storing data. Similar laws are already underway in Australia. These laws, willy nilly, will create data colonies and make it possible to share locally-generated information within local borders. Tomorrow, governments may even ask data-generating players to locate themselves within their borders.

Despite the outcry that such data localisation attempts will throttle the democratic internet, many countries are going ahead with their plans. More will join them tomorrow. All with an eye on populism and political dividends. Just imagine if such parochialism pervades the internet, how concentrated will be data in few hands and how deep will be information inequality in the post-pandemic scenario.

If the champions of data localisation are allowed to have their way, they may succeed in checking unwanted surveillance. But, that will doubly harm the internet if, on the top of it, national data flows are taxed.

Will such taxation moves stop with directing more revenues into government coffers? No, they will not. They will also restrict governments by building walls around their data. That is sure to localise not just the data, the internet as well. In the bargain, creating digital dictatorships and data tyrannies.

The danger then is real. Digital dictatorships will use all localised data and information for their political interests and partisan designs. Certainly, it will not be in the interest of democracy and data rights of citizens.

There is a silver lining here though. Fear of digital dictatorships may facilitate the widespread commercial launch of personal web servers. These personal servers will allow individuals to store, share and publish information on the web or on their home networks.

These servers will be controlled by individuals to serve their own needs in stark contrast to web servers operated by third parties. That should ensure every individual enjoys control over his personal information.

When such personal web servers become a universal reality, websites can be set up and administered by individual internet users. That could well be the beginning of a new chapter in internet democracy, scalability limitations of personal web servers notwithstanding.

19 Patriotism on a Plate

It takes a pandemic to stoke the embers of gastropatriotism. Soon, they will develop into misplaced culinary jingoism.

Call it whatever, such jingoism will threaten the concept of common markets and currency unions. Some food economists explain this intake introvertism as a serious manifestation of the desire for self-dependence. As Covid warriors raise their battle cries for fighting against the virus on all fronts, they are pointing fingers at the pathogen for this surging food nationalism.

Whatever, blind nationalism will finally make its way to the dining table, the unlikeliest of places. Governments across the world are already using the pandemic as an excuse to drum up support for their food protectionist moves.

These governments will equate consumption of local products with patriotism and regional food security with nationalism. Such a show of skewed food nationalism may throw the concept of common markets out of kilter. Will that bother the nations concerned?

The writing is already there on the wall. France is going ahead nonchalantly invoking agroeconomic patriotism. This de Gaulle nation seems to be not believing in delegating its food supply to others. It is asking its people to buy French veggies though they are more expensive than other European varieties.

Well, tomorrow, the French government may ask all its retail chains to get their food supplies from local farms. It may infuse covert nationalism into its food courts by clamouring for farmer protection. Who can stop that?

Not just France. Poland is looking at dairy imports with disapproval. Trying to be a food patriot, Austria is toying with the idea of introducing regional food bonuses to help local foods tide over the pandemic crisis. Russia is slapping quotas on grain exports in a bid to restrict them. Vietnam is doing the same with its rice exports.

Such jingoistic moves are afoot in Greece, UK, Belgium, Bulgaria and Portugal. The list is long. This show of unabashed food nationalism will make food prices volatile and ram vulnerable importers over the economic precipice.

The culinary jingoism you see developing today is just a foretaste of the coming cloistered cuisine markets. Post-pandemic, such cloisterisation will certainly kill fair competition in common currency regions. Easy loans and eased antitrust rules will hasten that process, and tilt the level-playing fields in common markets. That is a no-brainer.

The inward-looking food origin labels will not help either. As they will be designed with an eye on discriminating against food imports, they will be required to show every metadata of the food – the makers, the ingredients and their origins, among other things. This is food racism.

Labelling protagonists may argue that it is necessary to fight the carbon imprint of food coming from outside. That is hogwash, if the labels are going to proclaim not just the nationality of the food product, but its regionality as well.

This sort of qualified and coloured patriotism, call it culinary parochialism, will eventually end up in gastroregionalism. For instance, beef from Burgundy, a region in east-central France, may not be allowed to go out of the region.

Or, Alphonso mangoes from Devgad in the Indian state of Maharashtra may not be permitted to move to other states in the country. That will be gastrochauvinism at its best. Worse, it may degenerate into gastroracism or some sort of culinary apartheid.

20 Socialisation of Debt

Not so long ago, debt was a desirable word. Corporate entities were piling on to debt to finance their mega plans and push up their shareholder returns, deftly avoiding debt traps on the way. That attitude towards debt may change post-pandemic. As companies see their cash flows enter the drought zone, they will struggle to service debt. Gasping for breath, survival and staying afloat will monopolise their minds.

Mounting stockpiles, dwindling customers, falling footfalls and retreating revenues will be hurting their bottom lines. To stop things from getting worse, they will be prepared to do anything, from selling divisions to stripping assets to divesting stakes.

As introvertism invades every social sphere and as deglobalisation becomes the norm in every business activity, debt too will change. Debt resilience will be the new corporate goal and staving off bankruptcy will be the new priority post-Corona.

Companies will go any length to acquire debt immunity. Particularly because the Corona crisis would have left heavily indebted companies brittle, ready to break at the slightest downturn. The fear of going broke will make the corporate sector victims of hurting debt phobia.

This dread of debt will make companies change the way they look at corporate finance. Companies will junk their yesteryear preference for debt as every crisis leaves the heavily indebted crippled.

Before Covid, cheap borrowings might have helped these companies churn princely profits and unleash a debt supercycle that put them through adrenalin shots. Tomorrow, it will not be that easy, perhaps not possible. With the end of the golden era of debt, indebted companies will struggle to avoid sinking into the recessionary quagmire.

Borrowing was pleasant when the going was good. Those very borrowings will turn into neck-breaking albatrosses as the going turns bad. Willy nilly, debt overhangs will throw even viable companies deeper into the vortex of bankruptcy.

The reeling economy will not be able to handle mounting debt defaults and bankruptcies among corporates. Many blue chip companies will go in for drastic restructuring to acquire the much needed resilience. As bankruptcy courts crack under the weight of claims, out-of-court settlements will become difficult.

Governments and central banks will toy with the idea of bailing out the corporate sector by favouring equity infusions over loan guarantees. Alongside, deep-in-debt companies will shut down divisions and sell assets to retire expensive debt. With so much debt on their books, innovation will be out of question for them.

With investments in innovative ideas not possible, corporate recovery will be delayed further. Unable to wait for that long recovery, corporates will gradually move towards loss-bearing equity. Debt will be out and equity will be in. In such a scenario, governments will be the only borrowing group in the market as they hunger for finance for their infrastructure projects.

As that finance gets hard to come by, governments will begin restructuring their debt. And exploring new avenues of finance. It is here that they may discover the beauty of social bonds that direct private capital for public good. As these social bonds are meant exclusively for social causes, they will play a major role in reconstruction post-pandemic.

This socialisation of debt will help governments to acquire immunity against Corona-caused shocks. The social bond proceeds may be leveraged to subsidise life-saving drugs and virus vaccines. They may be even used to insulate businesses from bankruptcies.

So, in all probability, social bonds may become the new norm in government finances, aiding the post-pandemic process of recovery and reconstruction. Social bonds may play such large post-Covid roles that even companies in the private sector could fall in love with them in due course. This will end governments' monopoly over issuing the new-normal social bonds.

Why, there could be even region-specific or project-specific social bonds over time, setting deglobalisation in motion even here. For instance, social bonds, styled as Corridor Bonds, may be issued to finance the under-development regional Delhi-Mumbai Industrial Corridor project in India, which will serve as a global manufacturing and trading hub on completion.

Or, social bonds, styled as Belt Bonds, may finance China's regional infrastructure project styled the Belt and Road Initiative, which is expected to shower economic prosperity on regions from Pakistan to China along the old Silk Road. Estimates say this project will bring trillions of dollars in infrastructure investments along and around the old Silk Road.

Given the importance of these regional projects to the respective nations and their nationals, private sector and public sector investors will not hesitate in subscribing to them. Post-Covid, such a participation will socialise debt, altering attitudes towards debt for ever post-Covid.

Also by Harish Kumar

Metaphoric Madness
Metaphoric Madness
More Metaphoric Madness
Much More Metaphoric Madness
Not The End of Metaphoric Madness

Standalone
Mega Projects Mega Realities
Canons of Corporate Surgery
Conspiracies of Colours
Politics of Eponyms
Who Took the Orange from my Rainbow?
Winking in Wunderland
The Post-Pandemic Planet

www.ingramcontent.com/pod-product-compliance
Lightning Source LLC
Chambersburg PA
CBHW071725170526
45165CB00005B/2164